TECHNIQUES FOR PROMOTING ACTIVE LEARNING

K. Patricia Cross

The Cross Papers
Number 7

March 2003

League for Innovation in the Community College

Acknowledgment

This guide draws heavily from the work of my colleagues, Tom Angelo and Claire Major, in two books:
Angelo, T. A., & Cross, K. P. (1993). *Classroom Assessment Techniques: A Handbook for College Teachers, Second Edition.* San Francisco: Jossey-Bass.
Angelo, T. A., Major, C., & Cross, K. P. (forthcoming) *Collaborative Learning Techniques.* San Francisco: Jossey-Bass.

The League for Innovation in the Community College is an international organization dedicated to catalyzing the community college movement. The League hosts conferences and institutes, develops Web resources, conducts research, produces publications, provides services, and leads projects and initiatives with more than 750 member colleges, 100 corporate partners, and a host of other government and nonprofit agencies in a continuing effort to make a positive difference for students and communities. Information about the League and its activities is available at www.league.org.

The opinions expressed in this book are those of the author and do not necessarily reflect the views of the League for Innovation in the Community College.

©2003 League for Innovation in the Community College

All rights reserved. No part of this book may be reproduced or transmitted in any form or by any means, electronic or mechanical, including, without limitation, photocopying, recording, or by any information storage and retrieval system, without written permission.

Requests for permission should be sent to
League for Innovation in the Community College
4505 E. Chandler Boulevard, Suite 250
Phoenix, AZ 85048
e-mail: publications@league.org
fax: (480) 705-8201

Copies of this monograph and past issues of The Cross Papers are available through the League's website at www.league.org, or by calling (480) 705-8200.

Printed in the United States of America.

ISBN 1-931300-35-6

Foreword

With each Cross Paper, K. Patricia Cross adds her seasoned voice to our continuing conversations on learning. Few authors, scholars, or practitioners passionate about the process of teaching and learning have her ability to so cogently and clearly outline practical strategies for teachers. In each of these volumes, she gets right to the heart of the matter of connecting with students and improving their learning experience in and out of the classroom.

Cross Paper Number 7, *Techniques for Promoting Active Learning*, is an engaging and practical look at what many in the education field consider the Holy Grail: active learning. In her own inimitable style, Cross demystifies the literature and clearly outlines key issues, suggested strategies, and basic procedures to promote active learning. Moreover, the volume is replete with useful examples and basic tips for integrating these strategies into your teaching practice.

Whether you're a first-time instructor, veteran teacher, or interested observer, you'll find Cross Paper Number 7 a useful tool to catalyze conversations on learning, develop innovative curriculum, or consider learning assessment models. We hope you enjoy!

Mark David Milliron
President and CEO
League for Innovation in the Community College

Techniques for Promoting Active Learning

K. Patricia Cross

The role of college teachers has shifted dramatically over the past decade, stimulated in part by the assessment movement with its assumptions of institutional accountability for student learning, and in part by major advances in our understanding of the learning process. Research and scholarship on cognition have demonstrated convincingly that learners must be actively engaged in building their own minds; teachers cannot simply pour their knowledge into the heads of students and hope that the added information will be assimilated by students into the understandings that we call learning.

The purpose of Cross Paper Number 7 is to present a brief and practical guide to a sampler of active learning techniques that can be used in community college classrooms to promote active learning.

While much of the literature on active learning emphasizes the value of collaborative and small-group learning, active learning does not always involve *inter*action. It must, however, be active, involving reflection and self-monitoring of both the processes and the results of learning. A highly skilled listener, which most students are not, can be actively involved in a lecture, for example, by self-questioning, critical analysis, and active incorporation of new information into existing knowledge. The integration of separate bits of information into a body of understanding is an active process that is sometimes called deep learning, as opposed to surface learning, which rests lightly in bits and pieces on the surface and is quickly forgotten.

This guide includes not only collaborative learning techniques (CoLTs), but also techniques such as the Punctuated Lecture and the Minute Paper that originally appeared as Classroom Assessment Techniques (CATs) (Angelo & Cross, 1993). Most CATs not only provide information to the instructor on what students are learning, but also help students remain actively engaged in assessing their own learning.

New Roles for Instructors

Embarking on active learning techniques is neither a high-risk venture in which all things familiar and comfortable about the traditional classroom are abandoned, nor is it something to be introduced spontaneously on a slow day to see what happens when the responsibility for student learning is turned over to students. If collaborative learning and other active learning techniques are to be successful, thoughtful consideration must be given to the host of factors involved in deciding how well the activity will serve the instructional goals of the course.

There are honest differences, forcefully expressed in the literature, about the appropriate roles for instructors in promoting active learning. Opinions run the gamut, from convictions that instructors should play a minimal role in shaping and directing the work of student learning groups to beliefs that instructors must accept responsibility to structure the learning tasks, monitor group progress, and intervene if students get off track. Some instructors see themselves as coaches, observing, correcting, and working with students to improve their performance; some prefer the role of facilitator, which implies arranging the learning environment to encourage self-directed learning; some use the term manager, emphasizing a sequential process of setting the conditions and managing the process to produce the desired outcomes. Still others favor the role of co-learner, emphasizing the social function of constructing knowledge. The terminology is more than semantics; it reflects a variety of self-perceptions of the new faculty position in the classroom. On one matter, however, there is virtually universal agreement: the new college teacher is more than a dispenser of information. There is convergence in the literature advising flexibility coupled with sufficient structure to assure productive learning toward articulated goals.

Thus, the role of the instructor in active learning includes these responsibilities: orienting students to the goals and purposes of active learning, making decisions about the size and operation of learning groups, assigning and structuring learning tasks, assuring active participation of all students, and monitoring and assessing learning.

Orienting Students

Students, like teachers, have responsibilities in active learning that are new and different from what they are used to in traditional education. Collaborative learning, for example, involves a major reorientation for students. MacGregor (1990) defines seven shifts that students must make in their orientation to collaborative learning:

- from listener, observer, and note taker to active problem solver, contributor, and discussant
- from low or moderate expectations of preparation for class to high expectations
- from a private presence in the classroom with few or no risks to a public one with many risks
- from attendance dictated by personal choice to attendance dictated by community expectation
- from competition with peers to collaborative work with them
- from responsibilities and self-definition associated with learning independently to those associated with learning interdependently
- from seeing teachers and texts as the sole sources of authority and knowledge to seeing peers, self, and the thinking of the community as additional and important sources of authority and knowledge (p. 25)

Structuring the Learning Task

Miller and her colleagues (1996) warn, "A common mistake of teachers in first adopting an active learning strategy is to relinquish structure along with control, and the common result is for students to feel frustrated and disoriented" (p. 17). There is a difference between structure and control. In traditional lecture-discussion classes, the teacher retains control of the procedures minute by minute, determining what is discussed, as well as when and by whom. In collaborative learning, the teacher structures the situation so that students can take control of the learning process.

Designing and structuring the task is all-important. The learning task should generally be open-ended, requiring critical thinking with supporting evidence or arguments, and be directed toward a learning goal of the course. The task may promote controversy, and often results in some type of group product. Careful attention should be given, of course, to assigning tasks that can be accomplished in the specified time limits (Bean, 1996, p. 152).

Most experienced teachers advise that in general it is well to move from more structure to less. Beginning students usually need and want more structure than advanced students, nonmajors more than majors, remedial students more than those who are well prepared.

Forming Collaborative Learning Groups

Size. While group size may be dictated by any number of factors and preferences, Bean (p.160) gives a cogent rationale for settling on five as the most effective size for classroom consensus groups. He observes that six will work almost as well, but that larger groups dilute the experience; groups of four tend to divide into pairs, and groups of three tend toward a pair and an outsider. Bean suggests, however, that long-range working groups, such as those assigned to write a report together, function best when they are smaller; three seems optimal. Smith (1996) prefers to keep groups small (two or three), particularly in the beginning, in order to maximize involvement, and of course there are many times when pairs work best. This is especially the case in quick exchanges such as an interrupted lecture, where minimal disruption in the physical formation of the group is desired. In laboratory work, computer assignments, and other forms of cooperative learning, the size of the group may be dictated by the arrangement of physical facilities.

Physical Arrangements. Collaborative learning can be done in a variety of physical settings, from large lecture halls to distance learning to laboratories. The techniques described in this guide lend themselves to use in the average classroom. Using neighboring pairs of students to exchange viewpoints and information can be done in large classes as well as small. Most classrooms will accommodate a limited number of four- or five-member groups, but for some faculty and students, the noise level generated in a classroom where students are participating fully in lively discussions is likely to be disruptive, especially compared with the order and quiet of the well-managed traditional classroom. Despite the noise, however, Bean (1996) advises keeping all groups in the classroom rather than dispersing them to hallways or other rooms. In fact, he claims, "The loud hum in the room actually stimulates participation and draws groups together in tight circles" (p. 153). There are, however, no hard and fast rules about this; instructors will do what works for them.

Group Constituency. There appears to be a consensus developing that instructors should assign students to groups unless there is some specific reason for letting students choose their own groups. Permitting students to select their own groups often leads to groups based on friendships, and discussion may wander away from the task at hand. Moreover, self-selected groups may deny students the opportunity to learn from diverse viewpoints and perspectives. Exposing students to ideas and people that they may not have met before is a major educational value of collaborative learning.

Research on diversity in cognitive style shows that diverse groups are more productive than homogeneous groups, but the downside is that students are often less satisfied. Thus, some authors conclude that "teachers are faced with a difficult trade-off when they form groups: cognitive diversity increases group conflict and thus decreases satisfaction, but it also increases performance" (Miller, 1994, p. 38). Excessive conflict, of course, decreases performance, but so does excessive harmony when group members have no opposing points of view to challenge their thinking. The important point to keep in mind is that there are many forms of diversity–ethnicity, age, experience, cognitive style, academic major, grades (overall or on a recent test), and gender, to name a few. How groups are constituted for optimal balance between productivity, harmony, and satisfaction will depend on the goals of the course and the learning tasks that are assigned.

USING THIS GUIDE

The concept of active learning has more research support than any other teaching or learning practice (Slavin, 1989-90; Johnson, Johnson, & Smith, 1991). ERIC lists more than 6,000 articles written by researchers, scholars, and experienced classroom teachers on the art and science of active learning. This guide is merely an introduction to this vast work, and should be viewed as a sampler of techniques devised by creative teachers from K-12 through research universities.

The techniques were selected with two criteria in mind: 1) they are applicable across a wide range of disciplines and classrooms, and 2) they are practical and easy to manage. I encourage you to use your own creativity in adapting the techniques to your particular course goals and teaching style.

1. GOAL AND SYLLABUS REVIEW

Description and Purpose. Students list or rate their learning goals for the course. The purpose of asking students to define their learning goals during the first week of class is to improve student motivation and acceptance of responsibility by making them conscious of what they hope to accomplish in the class.

Procedure. Before you begin, define your own learning goals for the class. Ask students to write out three to five personal learning goals they hope to accomplish during the course, or hand out the syllabus or a simple form with course goals listed and ask students to rate their relative importance. Use class discussion of goals to identify, clarify, and modify course goals.

Example. An instructor in automobile technology found that most students listed very specific practical goals. However, he had two further goals for the course that he thought were important: 1) to learn to stay current in skills and knowledge in the rapidly changing field of auto repair, and 2) to develop skill and confidence in explaining diagnoses and planned repairs to customers. He invited students to respond to the importance of these goals through class discussion.

Variation. Use this technique as an opportunity for a more lively and involved review of the syllabus. On the first day of class, pass out the syllabus and ask students to meet in groups to generate questions about it.

This technique may also be used to introduce a single learning unit. Asking students to generate questions about a reading assignment encourages reading the assignment before class.

Tips. Decide what might be negotiable. If student goals differ widely from course goals, how willing are you to change or modify course goals?

Give some thought to how students can realize more personal goals through special projects or term papers.

References and Related Information
Angelo, T. A., & Cross, K. P. (1993). See "Goal Ranking and Matching," pp. 290-294.
Davis, B. G. (1993). See "Testing and Grading," pp. 239-251.
Millis, B. J., & Cottell, P. G. (1998). See "The Cooperative Syllabus," pp. 42-48.

2. Background Knowledge Probe

Description and Purpose. Background Knowledge Probes are brief questionnaires prepared by instructors for use at the beginning of a course or to introduce a new unit. The purpose is to help the instructor determine the most effective strategies for teaching a unit and to help students identify important focal issues in the context of what they already know about a topic.

Procedure. Prepare two or three open-ended questions or a set of short-answer or multiple-choice questions that probe students' existing knowledge, and write these on the board or present them in a hand-out. Make it very clear that this is not a test or a quiz, but rather a device to help students and the teacher identify appropriate starting points and make effective decisions.

Example. An electrical engineering instructor wanted to determine what his students might already have learned, through coursework or on-the-job experience, about measuring current, voltage, and resistance. He prepared a Background Knowledge Probe illustrating displays on five measuring instruments and asked students to write out the readings for each of the instruments.

He found great diversity in the responses. Thus, he started the next class with a small-group warm-up exercise. He assigned students to groups of four and gave them 15 minutes to come up with the correct readings for all five instruments. This procedure capitalized on the advantages of peer tutoring.

Tip. Provide a mix of easy questions (to avoid frustration and build confidence and cooperation) and harder questions (to probe the level of background and understanding).

Make sure that the questions are related to what you really need and want to know about student background knowledge. It can be a frustrating experience for both teachers and underprepared students if student responses are at odds with teacher expectations. You will need to demonstrate to students that you are using their feedback to improve teaching and learning.

References and Related Information
Angelo, T. A., & Cross, K. P. (1993). See "Background Knowledge Probe," pp. 121-25.

3. Punctuated Lectures

Description and Purpose. After a portion of a lecture or demonstration, the teacher stops and asks students to reflect on what they were doing during the past 10 minutes or so and how their behavior while listening helped or hindered learning.

The purpose of this technique is to help students become more active and efficient learners by helping them self-monitor their learning.

Procedure. Select a defined 10- or 20-minute segment of a lecture. Decide in advance where you will stop the lecture. Then ask students to jot down what they were doing while listening to the lecture, noting how that behavior influenced their learning.

Example. After giving a lecture on the purposes of classroom assessment, a teacher of secondary education asked students to consider these questions:

- How fully was your attention directed to the lecture? Did you get distracted at any point? If so, how did you bring your attention back to focus?

- What kind of notes were you taking? In what ways were the notes useful to you at the time? How would they be useful to you in the future?

- Did you raise any questions to yourself about the information you were receiving?

After giving students several minutes to reflect and jot down responses, the teacher collected the papers and studied them for insights and suggestions. At the next class session, which was on active learning, she used the data to illustrate student involvement and the importance of self-monitoring.

Tips. Use this technique several times during the semester to give students an opportunity to apply their self-reflections to their learning.

Ask students to save their written responses in a folder and to reflect on improvement over time.

Variations. Ask students to prepare two questions that they should be able to answer from listening to the segment and then to pose their pop quiz to a neighbor.

To improve note-taking skills, use the Punctuated Lecture to give students an opportunity to compare notes with a neighbor.

References and Related Information
Angelo, T. A., & Cross, K. P. (1993). See "Punctuated Lectures," pp. 303-06.
Bean, J. C. (1996). See "Use Cooperative Learning Groups to Help Students Listen to Lectures," pp. 170-172.
Johnson, D. W., Johnson, R. T., & Smith, K. A. (1991). See "Lecturing with Informal Cooperative Learning Groups," pp. 91-102.

4. MINUTE PAPER

Description and Purpose. The Minute Paper is one of the best-known techniques for promoting active thinking, as well as for providing both student and teacher with evidence of student learning over a single class period. It requires students to review in their own minds what they have learned, and it provides the instructor with immediate feedback on student perspectives of the class session. It also permits review of unanswered questions at the next class session.

Procedure. At the end of a class period, give students several minutes to write the answers to two questions:

- What is the most important thing you learned today?

- What important questions remain unanswered?

Example. A journalism instructor realized at the end of a class period that she had spent far more time than she intended on the decline of interest in general-purpose magazines. When she reviewed the Minute Papers, however, she found that the students had paid scant attention to the historical analysis that fascinated her and had listed, as most important, tips that would help them become more successful writers. She realized that she needed to continually point out the connections between the course material and the real world of journalism in the job market.

Variations. Allow a few extra minutes for students to discuss their Minute Paper responses with a neighbor.

When material is technical, as for example in mathematics and the sciences, it is sometimes useful to ask a single question: *What was the muddiest point for you in today's class session?* An occasional alternative is to ask for the most lucid point.

Tips. Make sure that the double purpose of the Minute Paper is accomplished: to require students to review carefully what they have learned as well as to provide feedback to the instructor.

Overuse will result in quick compliance without thoughtful review and synthesis in their words of what students have learned from that class session.

A quick review of the responses to the Minute Paper makes a good way to open the next class session.

References and Related Information
Angelo, T. A., & Cross, K. P. (1993). See "Minute Paper," pp. 148-58, and "Muddiest Point," pp. 154-58.
Mosteller, F. (1989). See "'Muddiest Point in the Lecture' as a Feedback Device," pp. 10-21.

5. Critical Debates

Purpose and Description. Critical Debate is a version of the classic debate structure, but one in which students assume, research, and argue the side of an issue that is in *opposition* to their personal viewpoints. It helps students move beyond a basic dualistic understanding of an issue (e.g., right vs. wrong) to a tolerance for and understanding of different perspectives.

Procedure. Select a controversial topic and state it in the form of a proposition. Ask students which side they most agree with, and then ask them to research and argue for the opposing side. Prepare the class for a debate through lecture, reading, and discussion. Schedule and conduct a debate.

Example. An education professor used Critical Debate to address the topic of English Only Instruction. She asked the students to acknowledge their positions on the following proposition:

Our state should pass a mandate requiring public schools to provide English Only Instruction to teach immigrant children to speak English.

Her state was facing this issue, so the topic had been the focus of much media attention. She prepared the class for the debate by taking 10 minutes at the end of a previous class to state the proposition, assign students to small teams representing the side *opposite* the one they had selected, and make a homework reading assignment. When students came to the next class, they met with their research teams to formulate their arguments. Each team then met an opposing team to present its arguments.

After a brief break, the instructor asked students on both teams to work together to draft major points of the issue from both sides. Class closed with a discussion about both sides of the issue.

Tips. Students who are not very comfortable with each other or the instructor may lose trust when asked to argue the opposite side. Therefore, this technique may work best later in the semester when class expectations and trust have been established.

Select a topic for which students are sufficiently familiar with the issue to take a preliminary position.

References and Related Information
Angelo, T. A., Major, C., & Cross, K. P. (Jossey-Bass, forthcoming).
Bean, J. C. (1996). See "Classroom Debates," pp. 176-77.
Johnson, D. W., Johnson, R. T., & Smith, K. A. (1991). See "Structured Academic Controversies," pp. 75-77.

6. JIGSAW

Description and Purpose. Jigsaw is helpful in motivating students to accept responsibility for learning something well enough to teach it to their peers.

Students work in small groups to develop knowledge about a given topic and to formulate effective ways of teaching it to others. Then these newly expert groups break up, and students move to a new group to teach their subject to their peers. Each new group thus consists of students who have developed expertise in different subtopics.

Procedure. The instructor selects a topic and respective subtopics for the class to investigate and discuss. Students select or are assigned to expert groups where the task is to master the content and issues, and to determine the best ways to teach the material to their peers. Students then split into new groups so that each student in the new group has studied and discussed a different subtopic with peers. Students take turns teaching the material or leading the discussion. The instructor may hold a full class discussion on the topic.

Example. Toward the end of the semester, an English instructor teaching a Southern Writers course decided to have her class examine the topic of how Southern writers often use people and events from their own lives as elements in their fiction. She selected five authors for the assignment: William Faulkner, Flannery O'Connor, Eudora Welty, Walker Percy, and Thomas Wolfe.

Each student selected one author to research in homework. At the next class, students worked in small groups to develop a list of biographical facts that appeared in the short stories of their author. They also determined how to teach the material to others. They then moved to new groups, each with representatives for each author. Students took turns leading the discussion. The professor held a class discussion and review session on the topic.

Tips. Assign homework so that students can study their subtopics before meeting with the expert groups. One way of assuring preparation is to test individually for content knowledge prior to the discussion in the expert group, with a retest administered based on after-group discussion. (See Number 11, "Test Review.")

Each person has a chance to be in the spotlight. Students take turns leading the discussion, so even students who are more reticent to speak up in class will assume leadership roles.

Cuseo (1994, p. 5) suggests that if this task is used for higher-order skills, tasks should be (1) ill-structured questions without an easy resolution, (2) issues to be discussed or debated, or (3) decision-making tasks requiring exploration of alternative solutions.

Because of its highly contrived structure, this technique should not be overused.

References and Related Information
Angelo, T. A., Major, C., & Cross, K. P. (Jossey-Bass, forthcoming).
Aronson, E., Blaney, N., Stephan, C., Sikes, J., & Snapp, M. (1978). *The Jigsaw Classroom.*
Millis, B. J., & Cottell, P. G. (1998). See "Reciprocal Teaching," pp. 125-148.

7. THINK-PAIR-SHARE

Description and Purpose. Think-Pair-Share is a very basic group technique that appears in many forms and variations in the literature on collaborative learning. After listening to a lecture, viewing a videotape, or reading an assignment, students think for a few minutes about a question posed by the instructor and then discuss their thoughts with a neighbor.

This technique provides students with the opportunity to brainstorm ideas and practice communicating them with peers; it tends to involve more reticent students who may take longer to formulate their ideas.

Procedure. Pose an engaging question or project to students about an assignment, reading, or lecture, giving students time to think about the question before pairing with another student. Pairs then create a joint response, building on each other's ideas. Pairs may be expanded to quads, and finally to a full class discussion.

Examples. To demonstrate the power of group work, during the first week of class, an undergraduate geography instructor posed this problem to students: *Draw a world map depicting major bodies of water, continents, and countries.* Walking around to observe, the professor noted that the maps were incomplete and out of scale. She asked students to form pairs to develop a new map together. The instructor noticed that the new maps were improvements. She then asked each pair to join another pair and to develop a new map. Again, the maps improved. Finally, the instructor distributed copies of a world map, asking student groups to compare the map they developed to the real world map.

A writing instructor who planned to have students write argument essays throughout the semester posed the following question to the class: *What makes a written argument effective?* A homework assignment illustrating several different examples of effective argument prepared students for thinking about the question. Pairing during the next class period expanded individual lists, and full class discussion developed criteria to be used in peer review and in grading student essays.

Variation. To help focus student attention on productive discussions in the course, early in the semester ask students to develop answers to the question of what makes a productive class discussion.

Tips. Developing good questions or a challenging joint project, as in the above map example, is all-important. If questions are narrow in scope, conversations will lag and think time will be nonproductive.

Be sure to allow enough think time before students share. Asking students to jot down responses in writing will discourage the temptation to wait and see what their partner has come up with.

References and Related Information
Angelo, T. A., Major, C., & Cross, K. P. (Jossey-Bass, forthcoming).
Millis, B. J., & Cottell, P. G. (1998). See "Beginning Structures," pp. 69-91.

8. Talking Chips

Description and Purpose. Students participate in a group discussion, surrendering a token or chip each time they speak. The purpose is to encourage participation from all members. Talking Chips encourages reticent students to speak out and talkers to reflect.

Procedure. Have students form groups, and give each student several tokens that will serve as permission to participate in the conversation. Students surrender a token each time they contribute or debate a point. Once all of a student's chips are down, he or she should wait to participate again until all tokens are down, retrieved, and redistributed.

Example. A precalculus instructor decided to form groups to work together for the entire semester. About two weeks into the semester, she noticed that while most of the groups were working well, one group was not. One student seemed to dominate the discussion, while other members seemed to accept his responses. The instructor felt that if she did not move soon, the group would have problems for the semester. She decided to try Talking Chips.

The instructor posed a problem for group work, emphasizing that she wanted participation from all group members. She gave each student several poker chips, informing them that they could make suggestions, pose questions, and support or refute a point made by another member of the group. However, each person who spoke would place a chip down in the center of the table. Once a student's chips were gone, he should wait to speak again until all chips had been placed in the center, collected, and redistributed to the group.

Variation. To assure that teams take responsibility for the learning and participation of all team members, assign playing card suits to identify students who will be called upon to present for the group. The instructor might, for example, call on students holding spades to respond on behalf of their team.

Tips. Use poker chips, paper clips, pencils, chalk, or other available items for tokens.

Make sure that the groups are given a structured task. A vague assignment will result in poor participation.

Talking Chips is most effective when used to deal with a problem, such as one dominating member in a group of quiet students or several dominant and clashing members in a group.

References and Related Information
Angelo, T. A., Major, C., & Cross, K. P. (Jossey-Bass, forthcoming).
Milis, B. J. & Cottell, P. G. (1998). See "Structured Problem Solving," pp. 95-101.

9. Structured Analytic Teams

Description and Purpose. Listening to a lecture, watching a video, and reading an assignment can be passive activities for students. One way to engage students more fully in the presentation is to form structured teams to discuss various aspects of the presentation.

Procedure. First, form student groups of four, giving each team one of these roles:

- Questioners – After the presentation, ask at least two questions about the material.
- Agreers – List the points you agree with, and state why.
- Naysayers – List points you disagreed with or found unhelpful, and state why.
- Example Givers – Give examples of concepts presented.

Then present the lecture, show the video, or assign the reading and give teams class time to prepare their responses. Then call on each team for an analysis.

Example. A professor in business management returned from a professional conference where he heard a stimulating, albeit controversial, keynote taking the position that business majors should be required to take more liberal arts courses. He played portions of the tape obtained from the conference for his class on leadership, and then asked students to form structured groups to analyze the arguments. After 15 minutes, he asked students to move to new groups consisting of at least one representative from each structured task to come up with a recommendation regarding requirements for the business major.

Tips. When time is limited, use only one group formation by assigning roles within the structured group so that each individual plays one of the roles.

Other roles might be assigned, such as summarizers, critics, or writers of exam questions.

References and Related Information
Angelo, T. A., Major, C., & Cross, K. P. (Jossey-Bass, forthcoming).
Bean, J. C. (1996). See "Designing Tasks for Active Thinking and Learning," pp. 121-132.

10. Everyday Ethical Dilemmas

Description and Purpose. With this technique, students are presented an abbreviated case study that poses an ethical question. They are asked to respond briefly and anonymously to the questions posed by the dilemma.

Everyday Ethical Dilemmas help students think through their values and give faculty information about how students make decisions about ethical behavior.

Procedure. Prepare a short case about an ethical dilemma, and pose two or three questions about it. As an in-class or homework assignment, ask students to take a position and write out their responses to the questions. Students meet in small groups to discuss their answers, and the discussion may be expanded to a full class discussion. (See Number 5, "Critical Debates" and Number 7, "Think-Pair-Share" for variations.)

Example. The instructor distributed a half-page case study about a college student, Anne, and her roommate Barbara. Barbara told Anne that she was planning to take her boyfriend's final exam for him in a required science course. The instructor asked students to respond briefly to two questions: 1) What, if anything, should Anne do about the plans that Barbara and her boyfriend have for cheating on the final exam? 2) Depending on your answer to Question 1, why should or shouldn't Anne do something? Discussion began in small groups of five students.

Variations. Involve students in simulation games wherein they play assigned roles in addressing ethical issues. Common simulations include mock trials, mock city council meetings, shareholder meetings, school board meetings, and counseling sessions.

Tips. Although ethical issues arise in every field and in daily life, the technique is easiest to use in preprofessional and professional fields such as nursing, social work, education, or business.

Cases of ethical dilemmas found in current news items help make the issues real to students, e.g., corporate finance, HMOs, political life, or college access.

References and Related Information
Angelo, T. A., & Cross, K. P. (1993). See "Everyday Ethical Dilemmas," pp. 271-274.
Davis, B. G. (1993). See "Role Playing and Case Studies," pp. 159-165.

11. TEST REVIEW

Description and Purpose. Students prepare for a test in small groups, take the test individually, and then retake the test in their groups. The purpose is to create an active learning group for a specified learning task while retaining individual accountability.

Procedure. First, students review for a test by discussing the material in small groups. They then take the test individually, submitting it to the instructor for grading.

Next, students form groups again–either original or new groups–to reach a consensus on the answers and submit a group response to the test.

Teachers may consider combining individual test grades and group test grades to determine individual grades.

Example. A psychology instructor offered a unit on cognitive learning theories. She used three class sessions for reading assignments, lectures, and class discussion, and then informed students that the next class session would be devoted to review and preparation for a half-hour, short-answer test on learning theories. Students were advised to come to the next class session with questions that they thought would be on the test, and to be prepared to discuss questions in a group session with four other students from the class.

The teacher administered the test in the first half-hour of the next class session, and after students had handed in their test papers, she asked them to again form groups of five to prepare a group response to the test. As expected, the group test scores were far superior to individual test scores. The instructor assigned individual grades on the cognitive learning unit by giving individual test scores twice the weight of group scores. Thus, a student who received a score of 70 on the individual test and a group score of 85 received a score of 75 for the unit.

Tips. To ensure individual accountability and group interdependence, average the scores from group and individual tests. You may wish to weight one more heavily than the other.

This technique can be used effectively for midterm and final exams.

References and Further Information
Angelo, T. A., Major, C., & Cross, K. P. (Jossey-Bass, forthcoming).
Johnson, D. W., Johnson, R. T., & Smith, K. A. (1998). See "Reviewing a Test," p. 74.
Davis, B. G. (1993). See "Testing and Grading," pp. 239-251.

REFERENCES

Angelo, T. A., & Cross, K. P. (1993). *Classroom Assessment Techniques: A Handbook for College Teachers, Second Edition.* San Francisco: Jossey-Bass.

Angelo, T. A., Major, C., & Cross, K. P. (forthcoming). *Collaborative Learning Techniques.* San Francisco: Jossey-Bass.

Aronson, E., Stephan, C., Sikes, J., & Snapp, M. (1978). *The Jigsaw Classroom.* Beverly Hills, CA: Sage.

Bean, J. C. (1996). *Engaging Ideas: The Professor's Guide to Integrating Writing, Critical Thinking, and Active Learning in the Classroom.* San Francisco: Jossey-Bass.

Cuseo, J. B. (1994). Critical Thinking and Cooperative Learning: A Natural Marriage. *Cooperative Learning and College Teaching* 4(2) 2-5.

Davis, B. G. (1993). *Tools for Teaching.* San Francisco: Jossey-Bass.

Johnson, D. W., Johnson, R. T., & Smith, K. A. (1991). *Cooperative Learning: Increasing College Faculty Instructional Productivity.* ASHE-ERIC Higher Education Report #4. Washington, DC: The George Washington University School of Education and Social Development.

Johnson, D. W., Johnson, R. T., & Smith, K. A. (1998). *Active Learning: Cooperation in the College Classroom.* Edina, MN: Interaction Book Company.

MacGregor, J. (1990). Collaborative Learning: Shared Inquiry as a Process of Reform. In M. D. Svinicki (Ed.), *The Changing Face of College Teaching*, New Directions for Teaching and Learning, No. 42. San Francisco: Jossey-Bass.

Miller, J. E., Trimbur, J., & Wilkes, J. M. (1994). Group Dynamics: Understanding Group Success and Failure in Collaborative Learning. In K. Bosworth & S. J. Hamilton (Eds.), *Collaborative Learning: Underlying Processes and Effective Techniques*. New Directions for Teaching and Learning, No. 59. San Francisco: Jossey-Bass.

Miller, J., Groccia, J. E., & Wilkes, J. M. (1996). Providing Structure: The Critical Element. In T. E. Sutherland & C. C. Bonwell (Eds.), *Using Active Learning in College Classes: A Range of Options for Faculty* (pp. 17-30). New Directions for Teaching and Learning, No. 67. San Francisco: Jossey-Bass.

Millis, B. J., & Cottell, P. G. (1998). *Cooperative Learning for Higher Education Faculty*. Phoenix: Oryx Press.

Mosteller, F. (1989). The "Muddiest Point in the Lecture" as a Feedback Device. *On Teaching and Learning: The Journal of the Harvard-Danforth Center* (April), 10-21.

Slavin, R. E. (1989-90). Research in Cooperative Learning: Consensus and Controversy. *Educational Leadership, 47*(4), 52-55.

Smith, K. A. (1996). Cooperative Learning: Making "Groupwork" Work. In T. E. Sutherland & C. C. Bonwell (Eds.), *Using Active Learning in College Classes: A Range of Options for Faculty* (pp. 71-82). New Directions for Teaching and Learning. San Francisco: Jossey-Bass.

About the Author

K. Patricia Cross

K. Patricia Cross is Professor of Higher Education, Emerita at the University of California, Berkeley, and Senior League Fellow at the League for Innovation in the Community College. Cross has had a varied and distinguished career as a university administrator (Assistant Dean of Women at the University of Illinois and Dean of Students at Cornell University), researcher (Distinguished Research Scientist at Educational Testing Service and Research Educator at The Center for Research and Development in Higher Education, University of California, Berkeley), and teacher (Professor and Chair of the Department of Administration, Planning, and Social Policy at the Harvard Graduate School of Education and Professor of Higher Education, University of California, Berkeley).

The author of nine books and more than 200 articles and chapters, Cross has been recognized for her scholarship by election to the National Academy of Education, receipt of the E. F. Lindquist Award from the American Educational Research Association, the Sidney Suslow Award from the Association for Institutional Research, and the Howard Bowen Distinguished Career Award from the Association for the Study of Higher Education.

Past Chair of the Board of the American Association for Higher Education, she has received a number of awards for leadership in education, among them the 1990 Leadership Award from the American Association of Community and Junior Colleges and the 1990 award for outstanding contributions to the improvement of instruction from the National Council of Instructional Administrators. She has been awarded 14 honorary doctorates and is listed in *Who's Who in America*.

Cross serves on the editorial boards of six national and international journals of higher education. She has lectured on American higher education widely in the United States and abroad in England, France, Sweden, Germany, the former Soviet Union, Japan, Australia, Hong Kong, and Holland. Her primary areas of interest are adult learning, changing college student populations, and the improvement of teaching and learning in higher education.

Cross received her bachelor's degree in mathematics from Illinois State University and her master's degree and doctorate in social psychology from the University of Illinois.

K. Patricia Cross
Professor of Higher Education, Emerita
University of California, Berkeley
Phone and fax: 510-527-9020
patcross@socrates.berkeley.edu
Mailing address:
904 Oxford Street, Berkeley, CA 94707